Date: 3/31/17

J 629.4 YOM
Yomtov, Nelson,
Sailing the solar system :
the next 100 years of space

SAILING THE SOLAR SYSTEM

THE NEXT 100 YEARS OF SPACE EXPLORATION

by Nel Yomtov

CAPSTONE PRESS
a capstone imprint

Graphic Library is published by Capstone Press,
1710 Roe Crest Drive, North Mankato, Minnesota 56003
www.mycapstone.com

Library of Congress Cataloging-in-Publication Data

Library of Congress Cataloging-in-Publication data is available on the Library of Congress website.
ISBN 978-1-4914-8265-0 (library binding)
ISBN 978-1-4914-8269-8 (eBook PDF)

Editor
Mandy Robbins

Art Director
Nathan Gassman

Designer
Ted Williams

Media Researcher
Jo Miller

Production Specialist
Katy LaVigne

Illustrator
Alan Brown

Colorist
Giovanni Pota

Design Element: Shutterstock: pixelparticle (backgrounds)

Printed and bound in the United States of America.
009679F16

TABLE OF CONTENTS

SECTION ONE THE DREAM OF SPACE TRAVEL

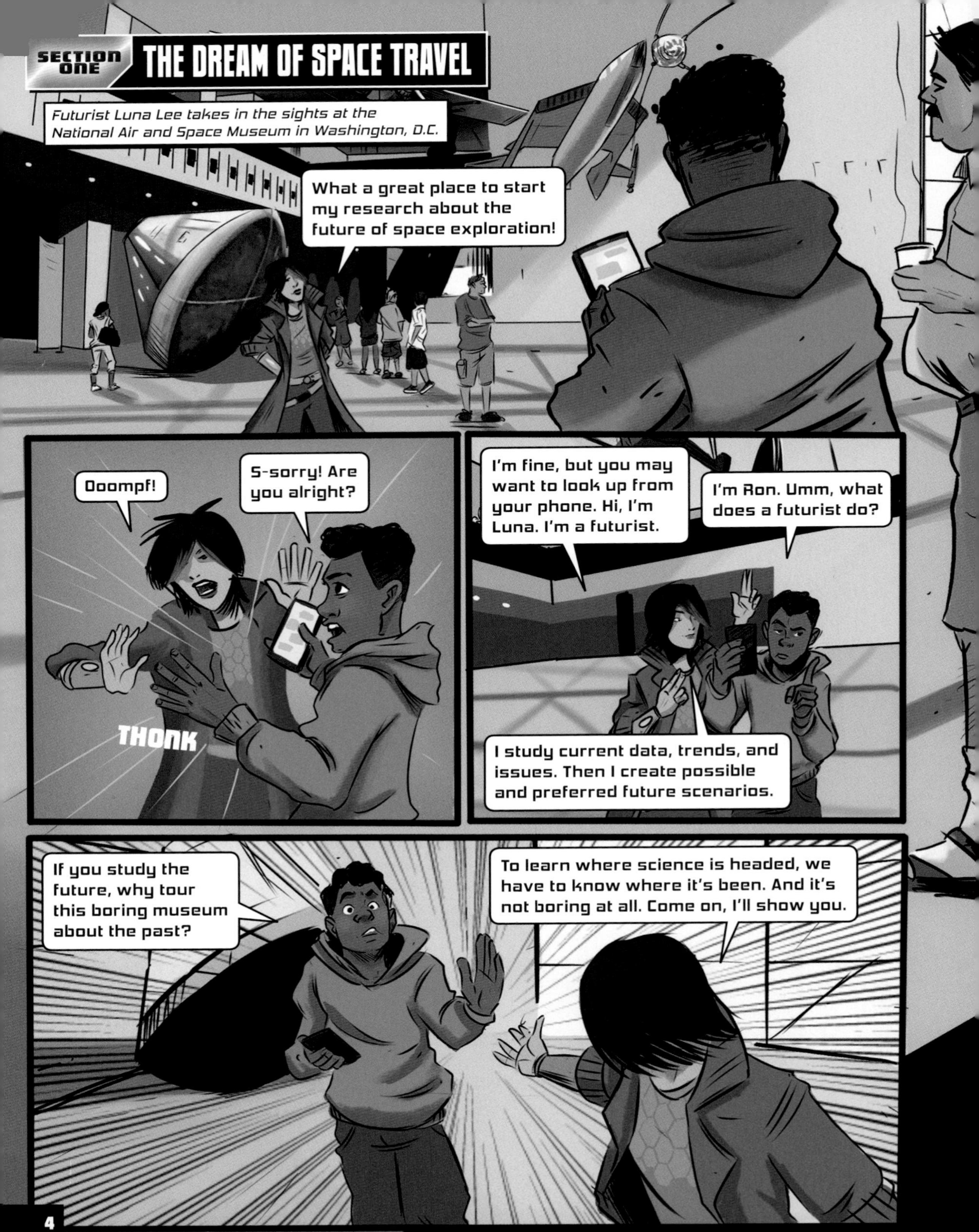
Futurist Luna Lee takes in the sights at the National Air and Space Museum in Washington, D.C.
What a great place to start my research about the future of space exploration!
Ooompf!
S-sorry! Are you alright?
THONK
I'm fine, but you may want to look up from your phone. Hi, I'm Luna. I'm a futurist.
I'm Ron. Umm, what does a futurist do?
I study current data, trends, and issues. Then I create possible and preferred future scenarios.
If you study the future, why tour this boring museum about the past?
To learn where science is headed, we have to know where it's been. And it's not boring at all. Come on, I'll show you.

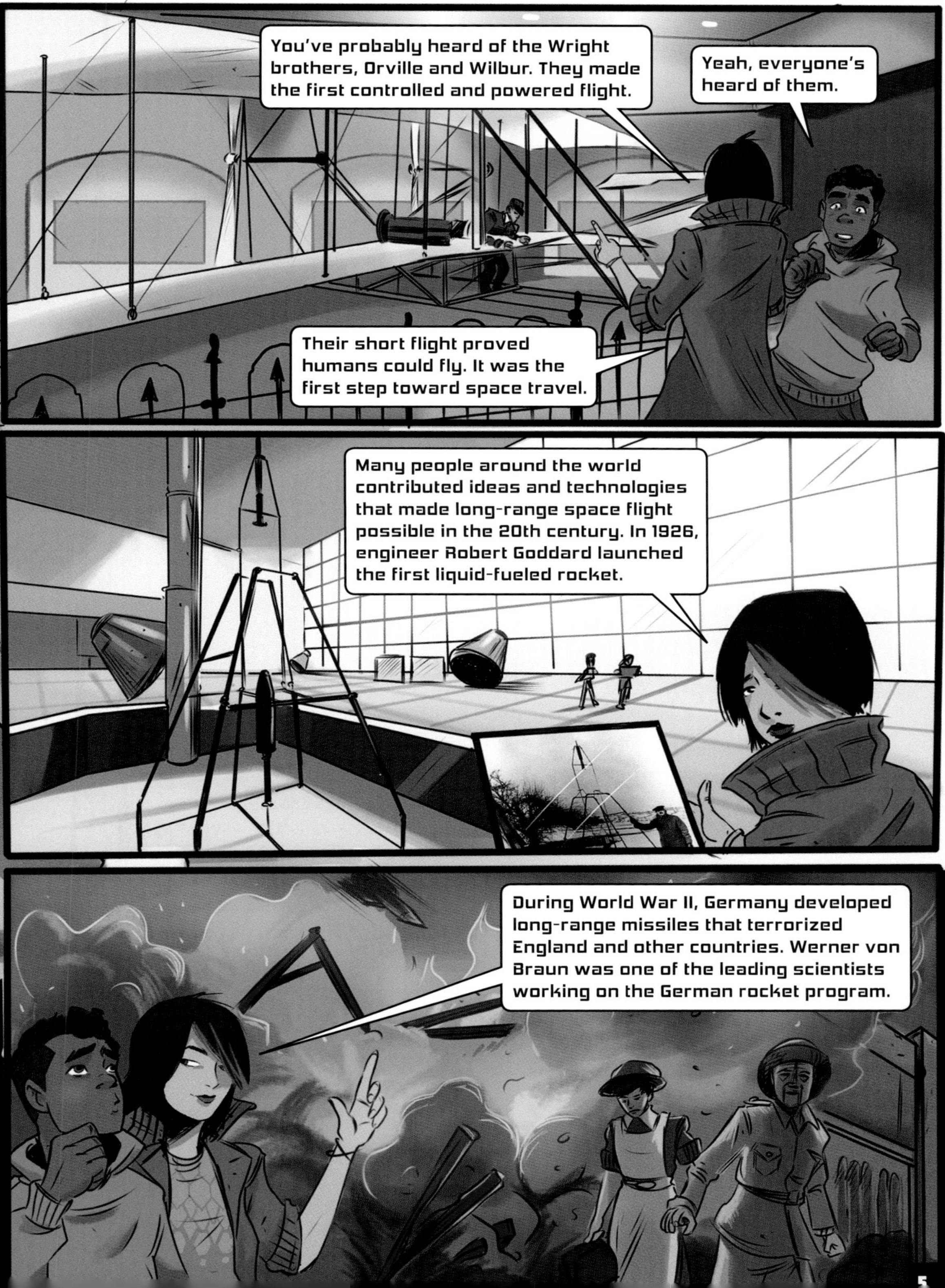
You've probably heard of the Wright brothers, Orville and Wilbur. They made the first controlled and powered flight.
Yeah, everyone's heard of them.
Their short flight proved humans could fly. It was the first step toward space travel.
Many people around the world contributed ideas and technologies that made long-range space flight possible in the 20th century. In 1926, engineer Robert Goddard launched the first liquid-fueled rocket.
During World War II, Germany developed long-range missiles that terrorized England and other countries. Werner von Braun was one of the leading scientists working on the German rocket program.

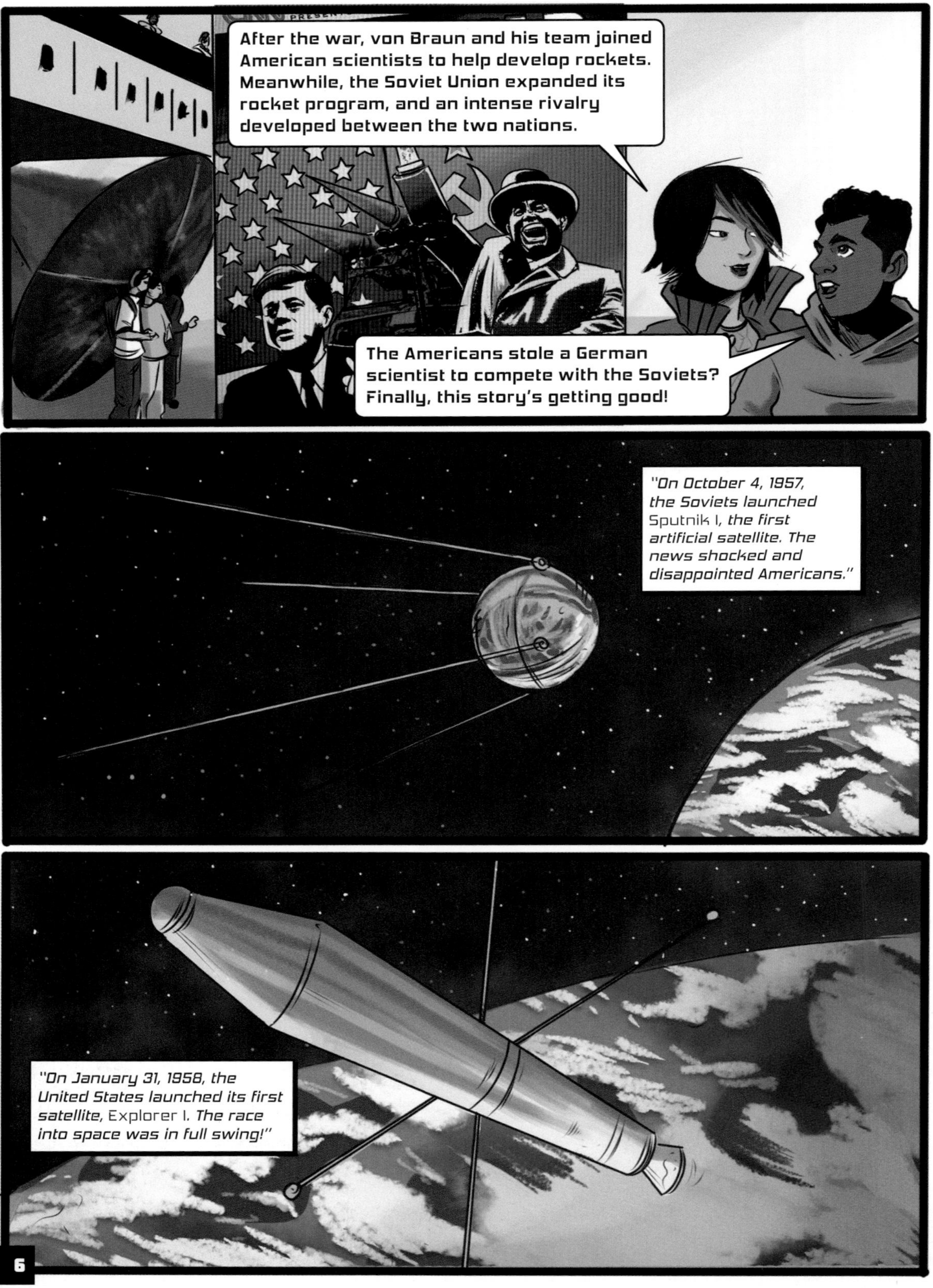
After the war, von Braun and his team joined American scientists to help develop rockets. Meanwhile, the Soviet Union expanded its rocket program, and an intense rivalry developed between the two nations.
The Americans stole a German scientist to compete with the Soviets? Finally, this story's getting good!
"On October 4, 1957, the Soviets launched Sputnik I, the first artificial satellite. The news shocked and disappointed Americans."
"On January 31, 1958, the United States launched its first satellite, Explorer I. The race into space was in full swing!"

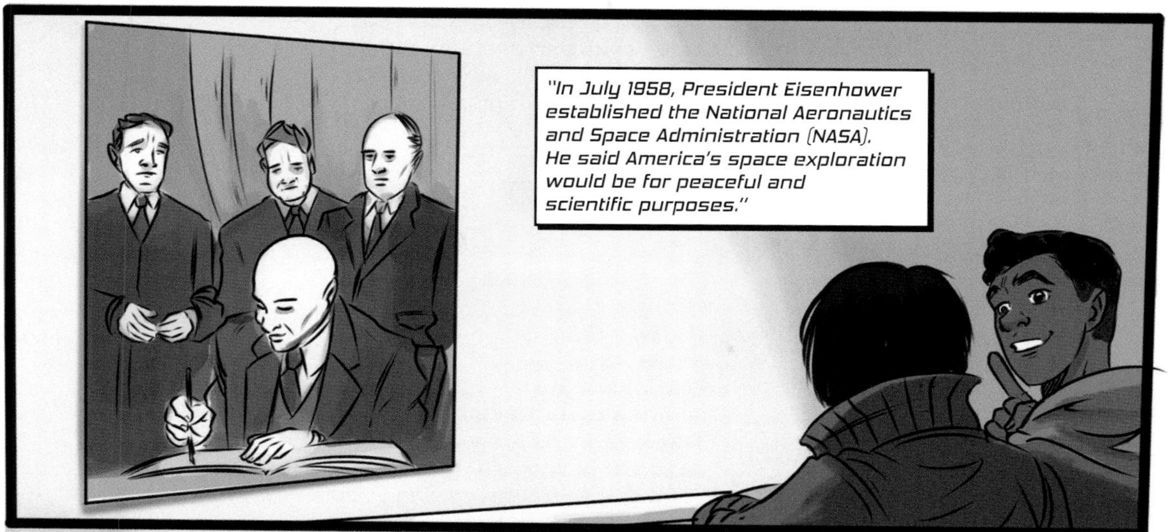
"In July 1958, President Eisenhower established the National Aeronautics and Space Administration (NASA). He said America's space exploration would be for peaceful and scientific purposes."

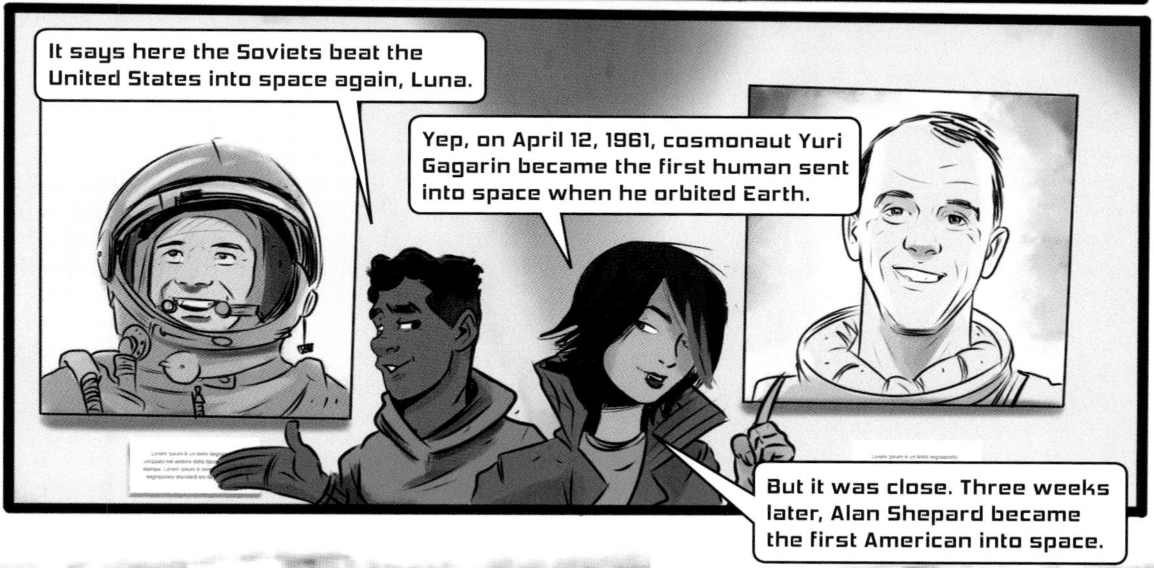
It says here the Soviets beat the United States into space again, Luna.
Yep, on April 12, 1961, cosmonaut Yuri Gagarin became the first human sent into space when he orbited Earth.
But it was close. Three weeks later, Alan Shepard became the first American into space.

SALLY RIDE

The Soviets sent the first woman, Valentina Tereshkova, into space in 1963. It wasn't until 20 years later that the United States sent the first American woman, Sally Ride, into space. On June 18, 1983, Sally made her historic voyage on the space shuttle *Challenger*. She flew two missions in 1984 and 1986. Sally went on to start her own company to help inspire young women to follow their interests in science and math.

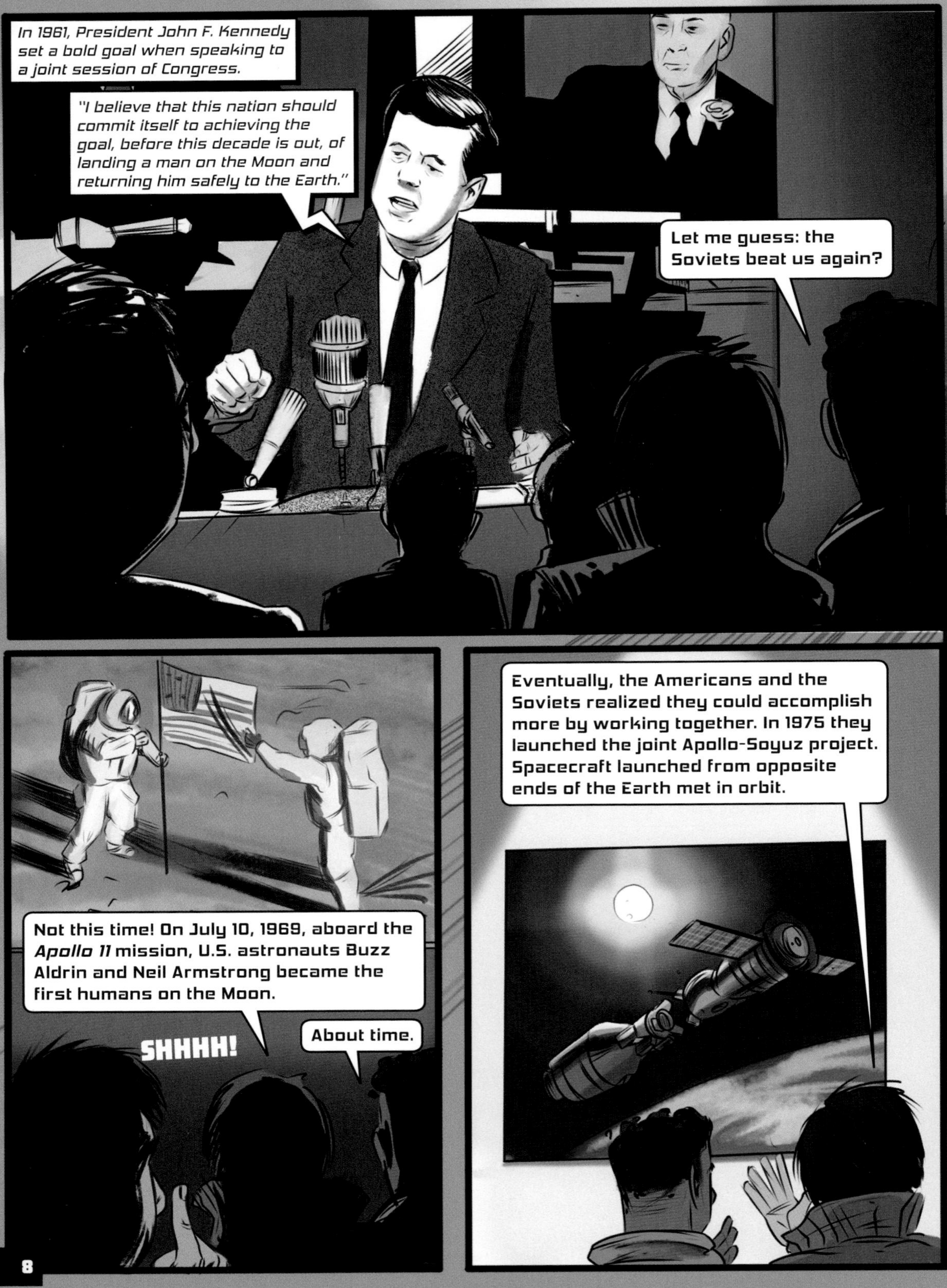

In 1961, President John F. Kennedy set a bold goal when speaking to a joint session of Congress.
"I believe that this nation should commit itself to achieving the goal, before this decade is out, of landing a man on the Moon and returning him safely to the Earth."
Let me guess: the Soviets beat us again?
Not this time! On July 10, 1969, aboard the *Apollo 11* mission, U.S. astronauts Buzz Aldrin and Neil Armstrong became the first humans on the Moon.
SHHHH!
About time.
Eventually, the Americans and the Soviets realized they could accomplish more by working together. In 1975 they launched the joint Apollo-Soyuz project. Spacecraft launched from opposite ends of the Earth met in orbit.

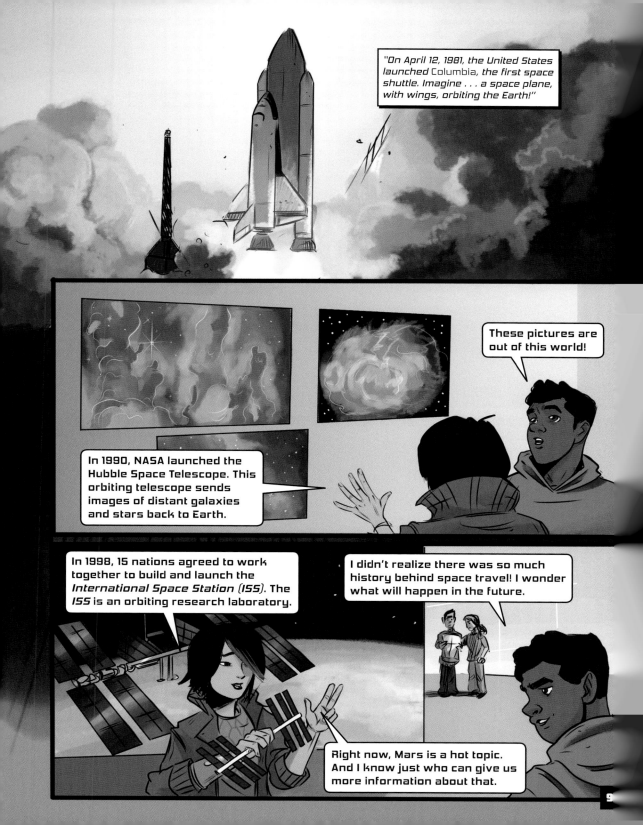

"On April 12, 1981, the United States launched Columbia, the first space shuttle. Imagine . . . a space plane, with wings, orbiting the Earth!"

These pictures are out of this world!

In 1990, NASA launched the Hubble Space Telescope. This orbiting telescope sends images of distant galaxies and stars back to Earth.

In 1998, 15 nations agreed to work together to build and launch the International Space Station (ISS). The ISS is an orbiting research laboratory.

I didn't realize there was so much history behind space travel! I wonder what will happen in the future.

Right now, Mars is a hot topic. And I know just who can give us more information about that.

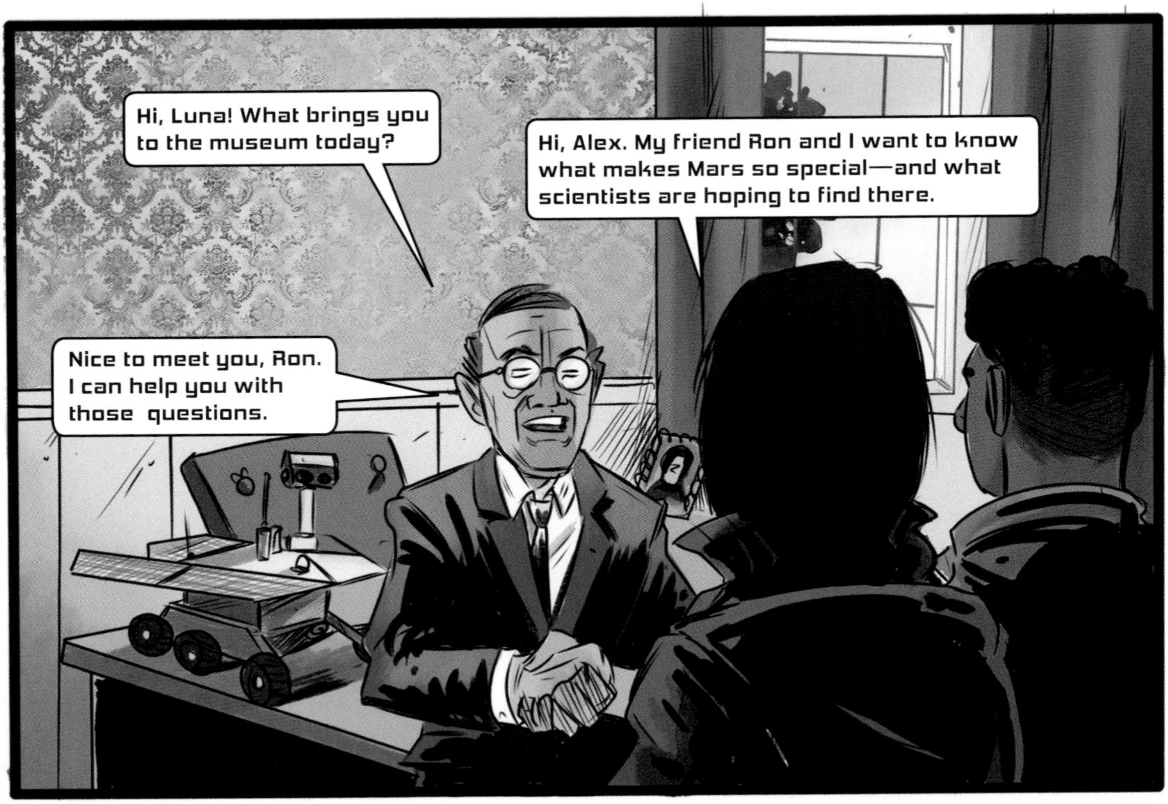
Hi, Luna! What brings you to the museum today?
Hi, Alex. My friend Ron and I want to know what makes Mars so special—and what scientists are hoping to find there.
Nice to meet you, Ron. I can help you with those questions.

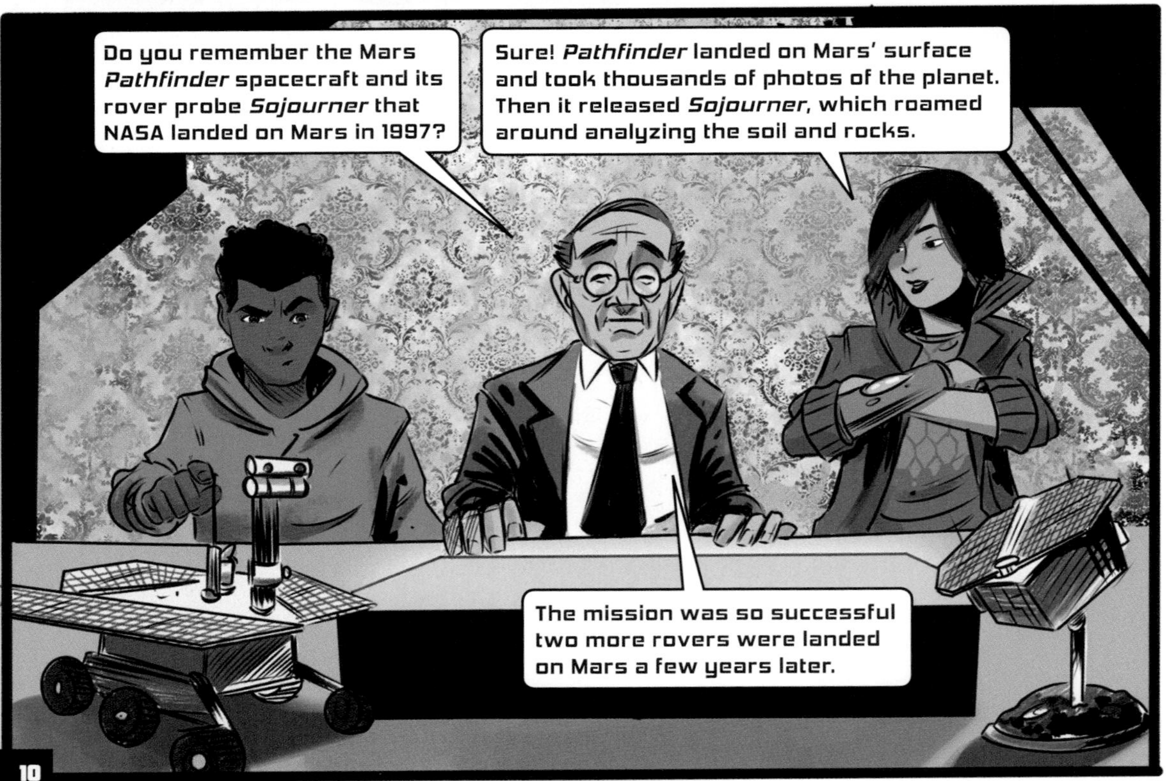
Do you remember the Mars *Pathfinder* spacecraft and its rover probe *Sojourner* that NASA landed on Mars in 1997?
Sure! *Pathfinder* landed on Mars' surface and took thousands of photos of the planet. Then it released *Sojourner*, which roamed around analyzing the soil and rocks.
The mission was so successful two more rovers were landed on Mars a few years later.

Mars once had liquid water in abundance. Water, of course, is essential for life.
If life can develop where there is liquid water, perhaps there was—or is—life on Mars.
So the search for life is one of the reasons for our missions to Mars!
The moons of Jupiter and Saturn also contain water, but they're very far away and too difficult to reach right now. Mars is close enough to Earth to explore.
Hmm. What if humans began living on Mars? That would give us the base we need to explore more distant worlds.
Many scientists believe people will have to live on other planets if the human race is to continue.
But how do scientists plan to explore Mars?
There are many possibilities. Let's take a look at one!

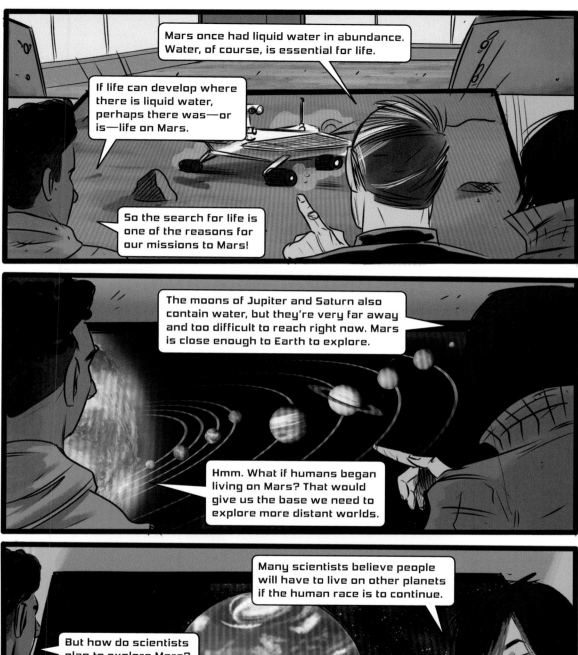

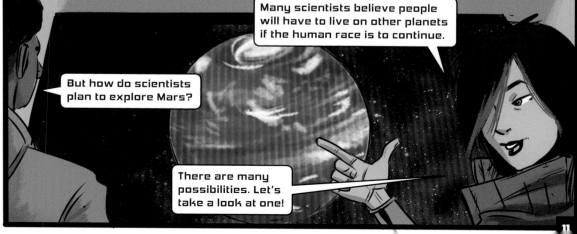

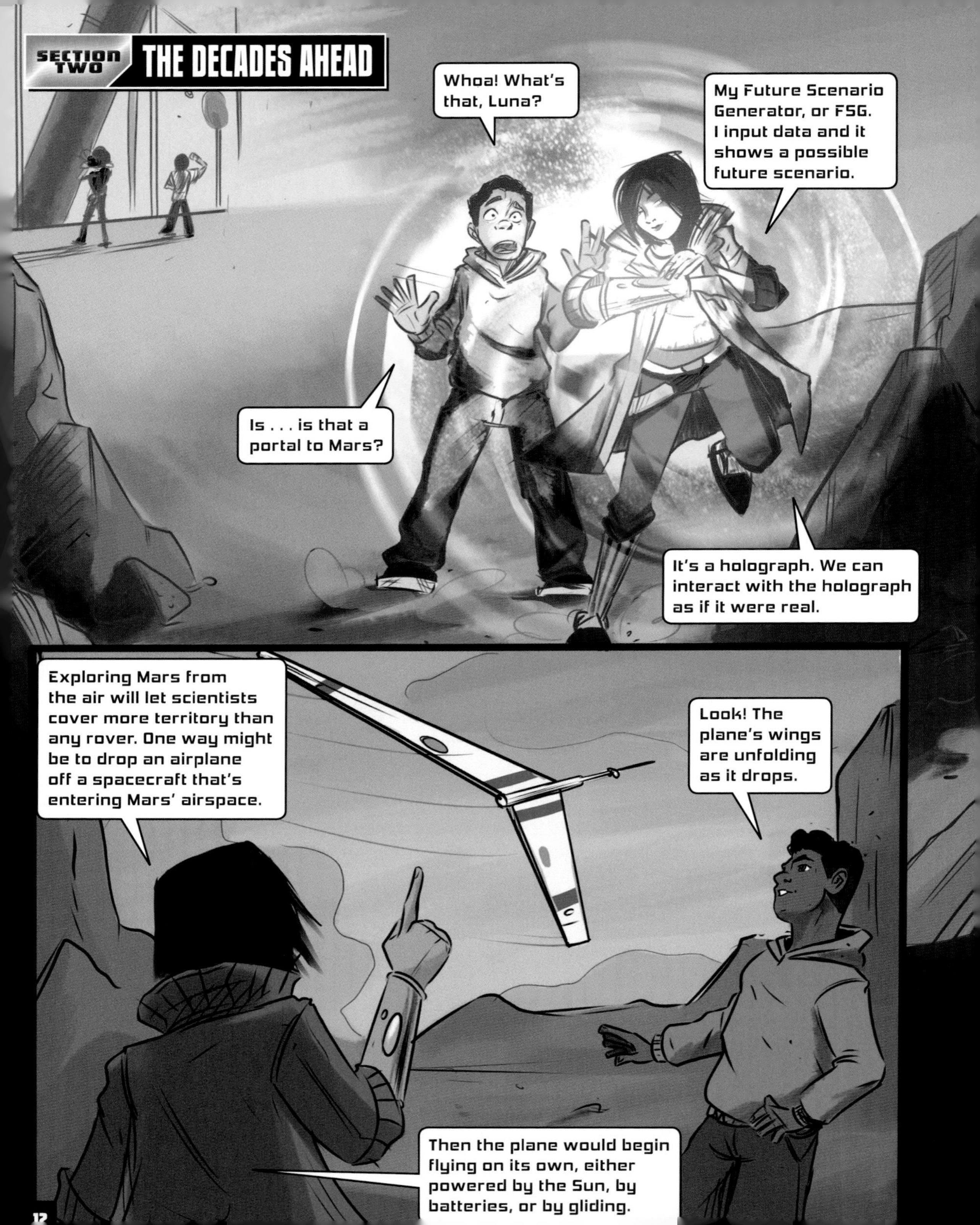
SECTION TWO THE DECADES AHEAD
Whoa! What's that, Luna?
My Future Scenario Generator, or FSG. I input data and it shows a possible future scenario.
Is . . . is that a portal to Mars?
It's a holograph. We can interact with the holograph as if it were real.
Exploring Mars from the air will let scientists cover more territory than any rover. One way might be to drop an airplane off a spacecraft that's entering Mars' airspace.
Look! The plane's wings are unfolding as it drops.
Then the plane would begin flying on its own, either powered by the Sun, by batteries, or by gliding.

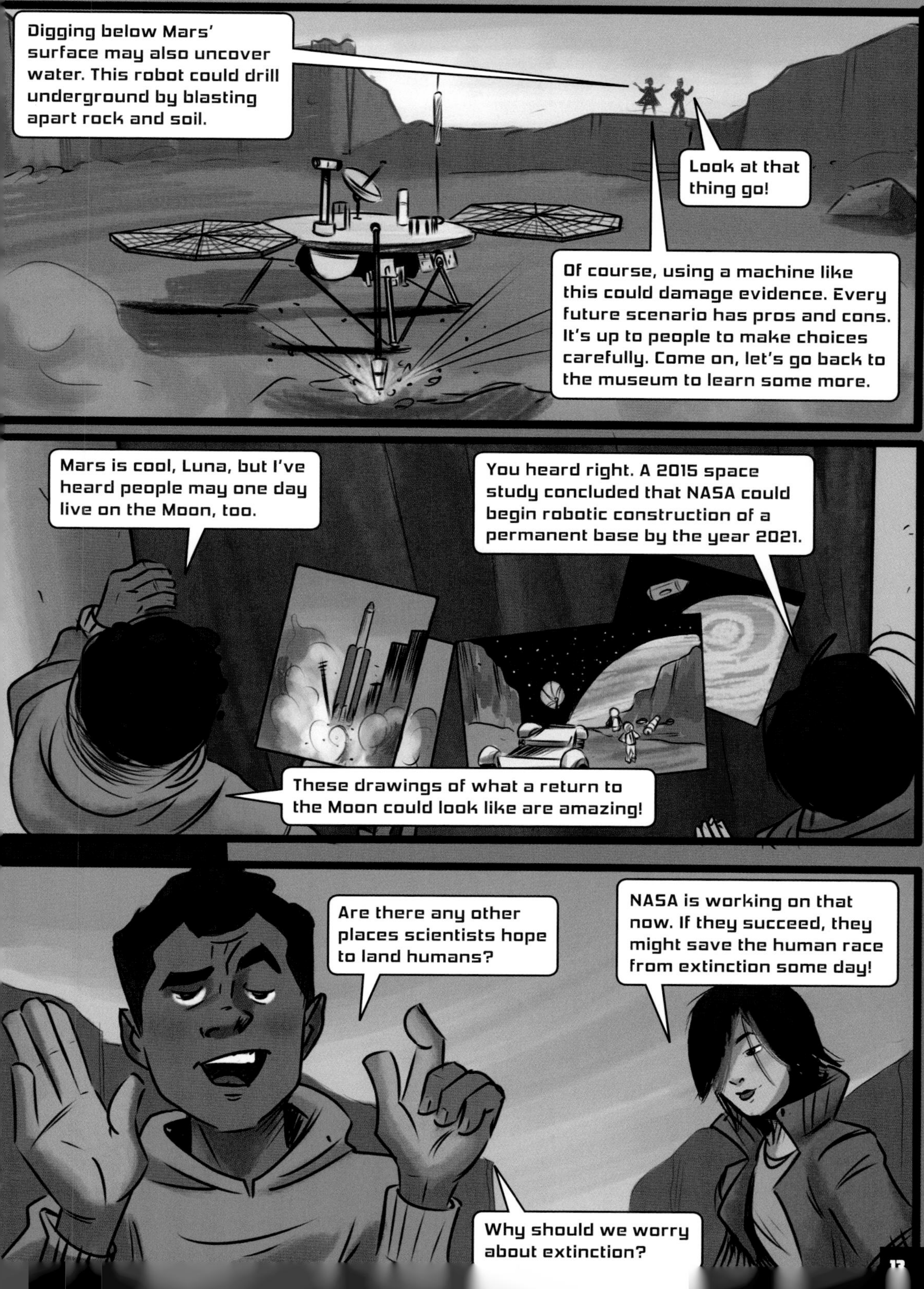

Digging below Mars' surface may also uncover water. This robot could drill underground by blasting apart rock and soil.
Look at that thing go!
Of course, using a machine like this could damage evidence. Every future scenario has pros and cons. It's up to people to make choices carefully. Come on, let's go back to the museum to learn some more.
Mars is cool, Luna, but I've heard people may one day live on the Moon, too.
You heard right. A 2015 space study concluded that NASA could begin robotic construction of a permanent base by the year 2021.
These drawings of what a return to the Moon could look like are amazing!
Are there any other places scientists hope to land humans?
NASA is working on that now. If they succeed, they might save the human race from extinction some day!
Why should we worry about extinction?

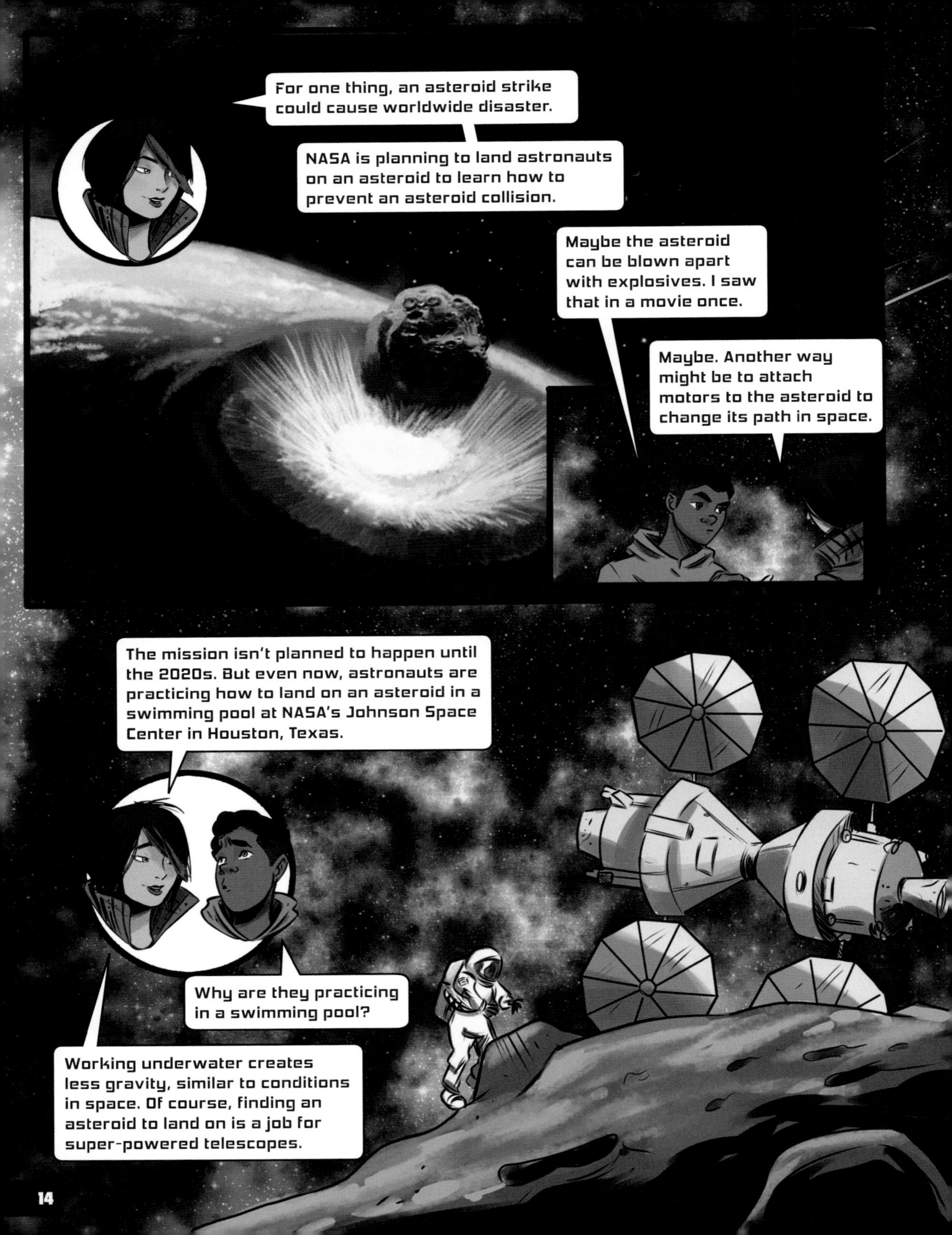
For one thing, an asteroid strike could cause worldwide disaster.
NASA is planning to land astronauts on an asteroid to learn how to prevent an asteroid collision.
Maybe the asteroid can be blown apart with explosives. I saw that in a movie once.
Maybe. Another way might be to attach motors to the asteroid to change its path in space.
The mission isn't planned to happen until the 2020s. But even now, astronauts are practicing how to land on an asteroid in a swimming pool at NASA's Johnson Space Center in Houston, Texas.
Why are they practicing in a swimming pool?
Working underwater creates less gravity, similar to conditions in space. Of course, finding an asteroid to land on is a job for super-powered telescopes.

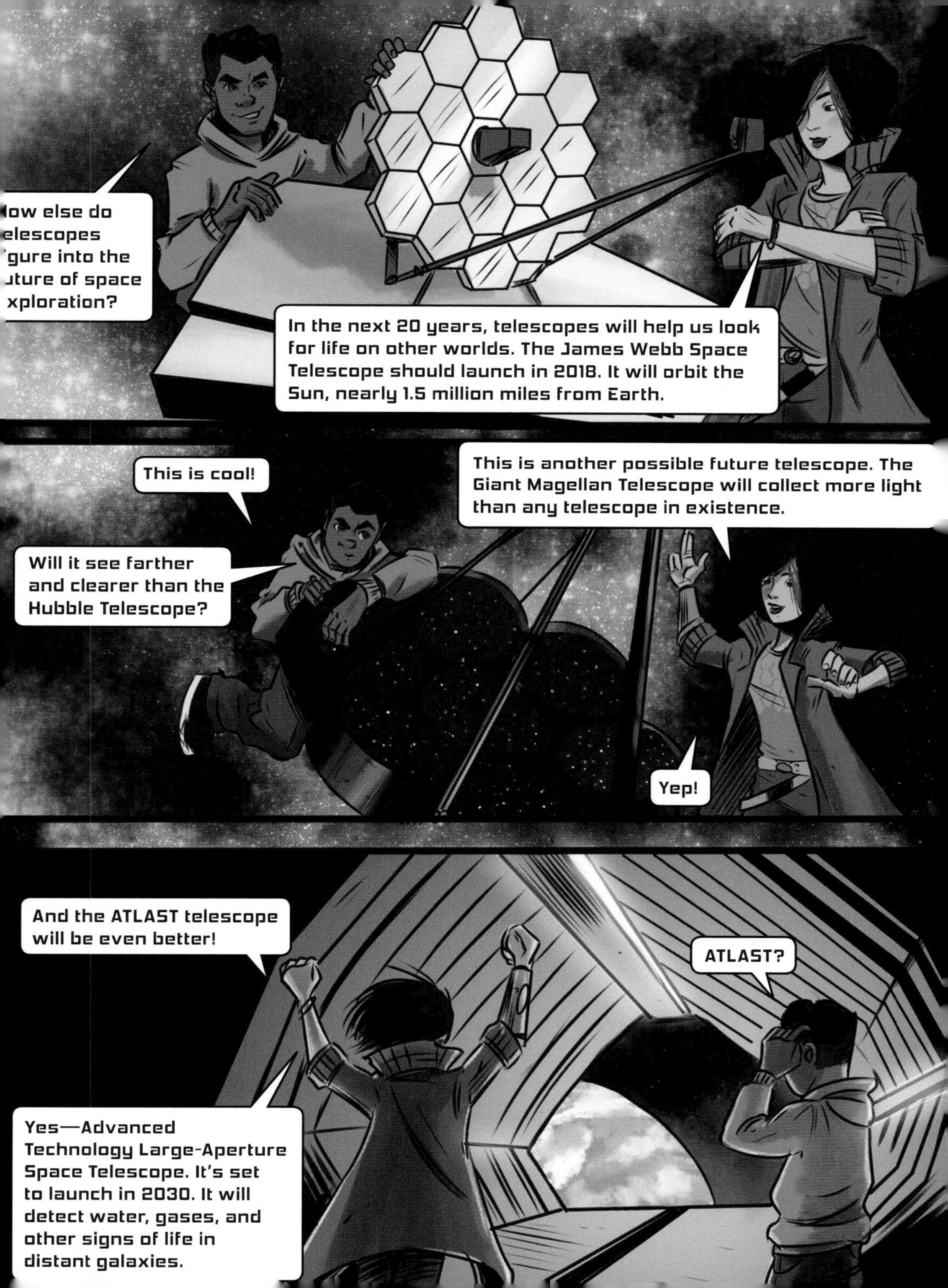

ow else do elescopes gure into the uture of space xploration?
In the next 20 years, telescopes will help us look for life on other worlds. The James Webb Space Telescope should launch in 2018. It will orbit the Sun, nearly 1.5 million miles from Earth.
This is cool!
This is another possible future telescope. The Giant Magellan Telescope will collect more light than any telescope in existence.
Will it see farther and clearer than the Hubble Telescope?
Yep!
And the ATLAST telescope will be even better!
ATLAST?
Yes—Advanced Technology Large-Aperture Space Telescope. It's set to launch in 2030. It will detect water, gases, and other signs of life in distant galaxies.

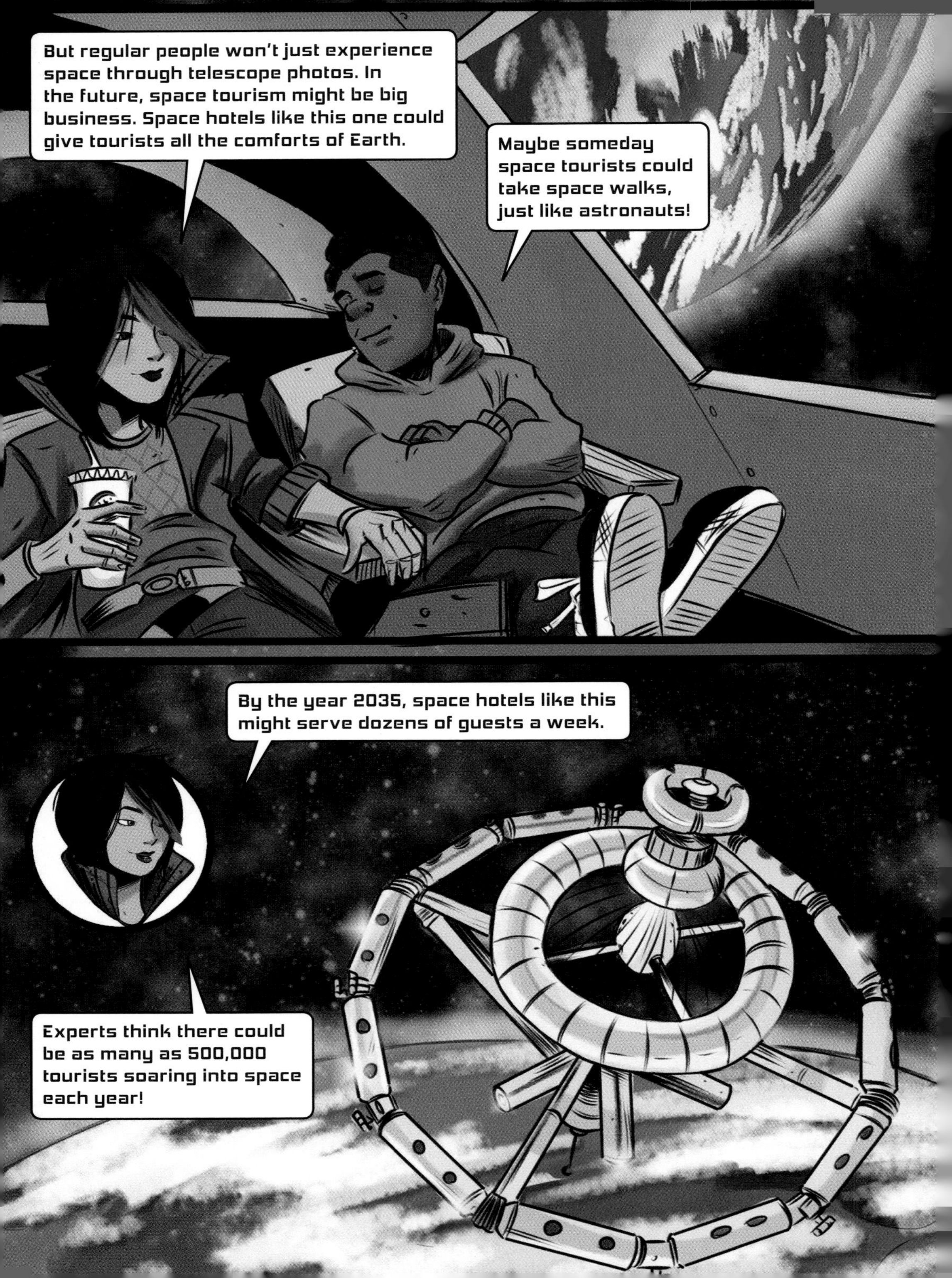

But regular people won't just experience space through telescope photos. In the future, space tourism might be big business. Space hotels like this one could give tourists all the comforts of Earth.
Maybe someday space tourists could take space walks, just like astronauts!
By the year 2035, space hotels like this might serve dozens of guests a week.
Experts think there could be as many as 500,000 tourists soaring into space each year!

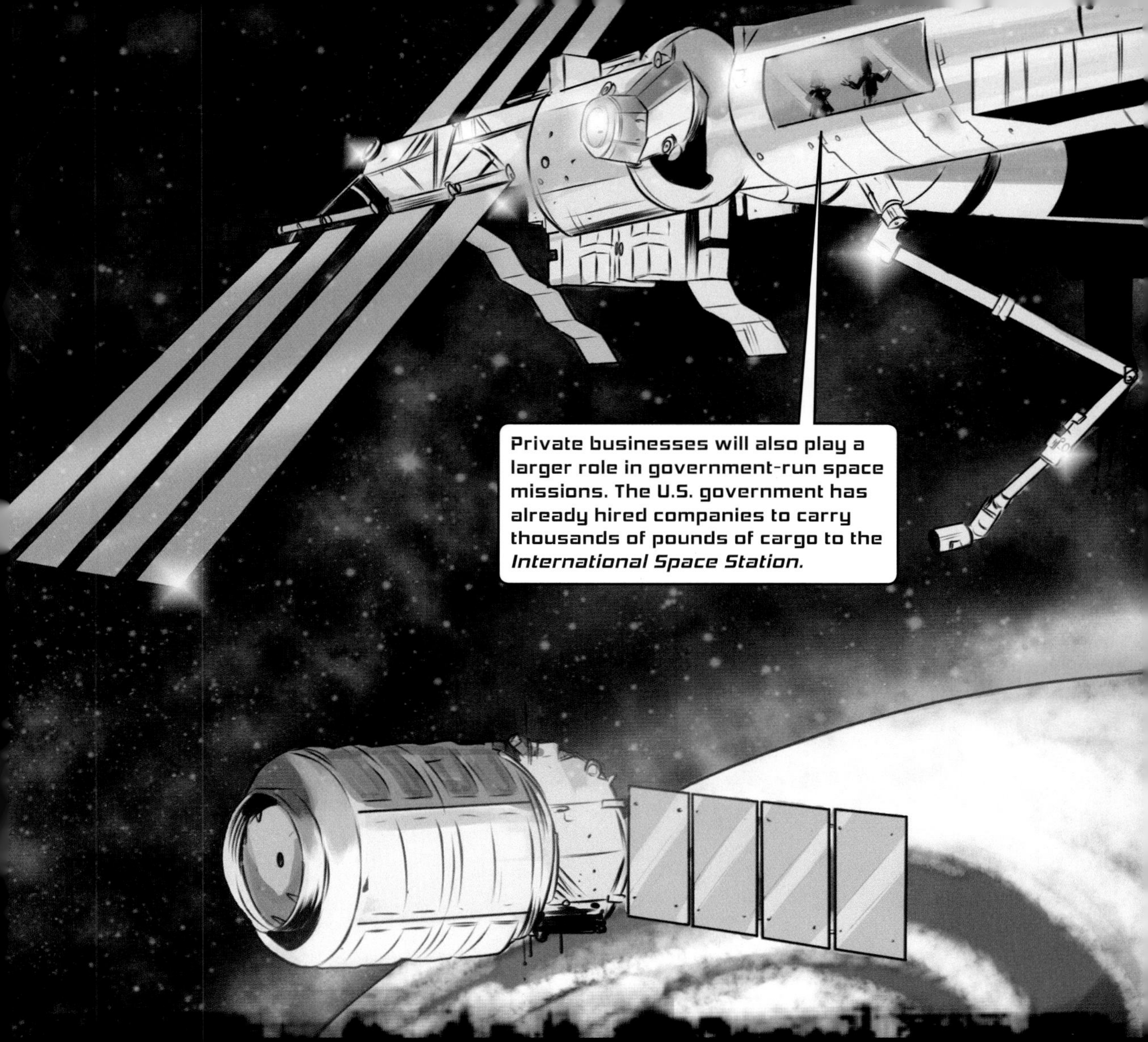
Private businesses will also play a larger role in government-run space missions. The U.S. government has already hired companies to carry thousands of pounds of cargo to the *International Space Station*.

THE HIGH COST OF SPACE TOURISM

From 2001 to 2009, eight private citizens each paid $20 million to travel to space aboard missions conducted by the Russian government. By 2014, the private space company Virgin Galactic had sold 700 tickets costing $200,000 each to fly into space aboard the company's rocket plane. The voyage will take passengers about 62 miles (100 km) above Earth. The tickets include three days of space training.

SECTION THREE THE YEAR 2120

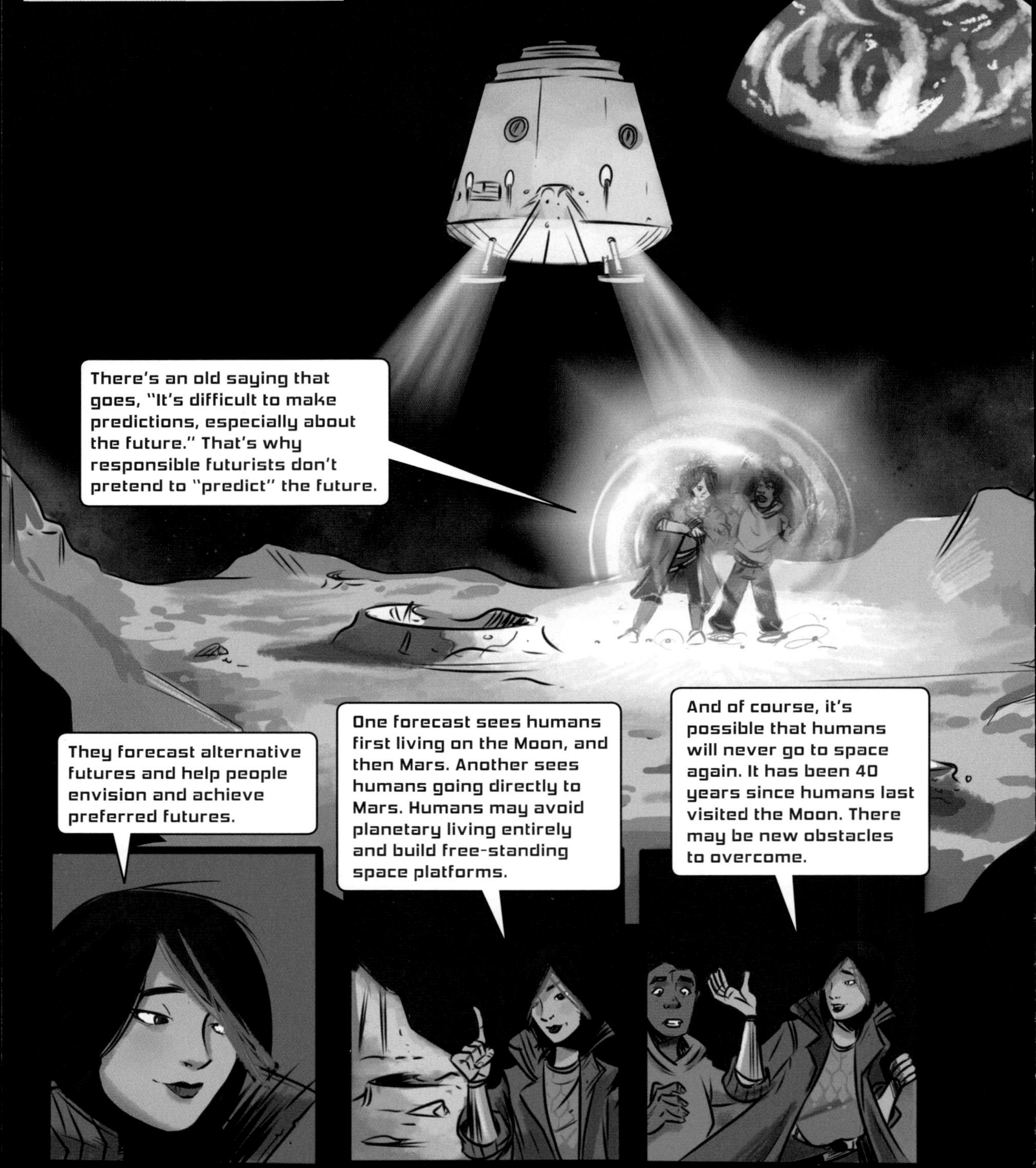
There's an old saying that goes, "It's difficult to make predictions, especially about the future." That's why responsible futurists don't pretend to "predict" the future.
They forecast alternative futures and help people envision and achieve preferred futures.
One forecast sees humans first living on the Moon, and then Mars. Another sees humans going directly to Mars. Humans may avoid planetary living entirely and build free-standing space platforms.
And of course, it's possible that humans will never go to space again. It has been 40 years since humans last visited the Moon. There may be new obstacles to overcome.

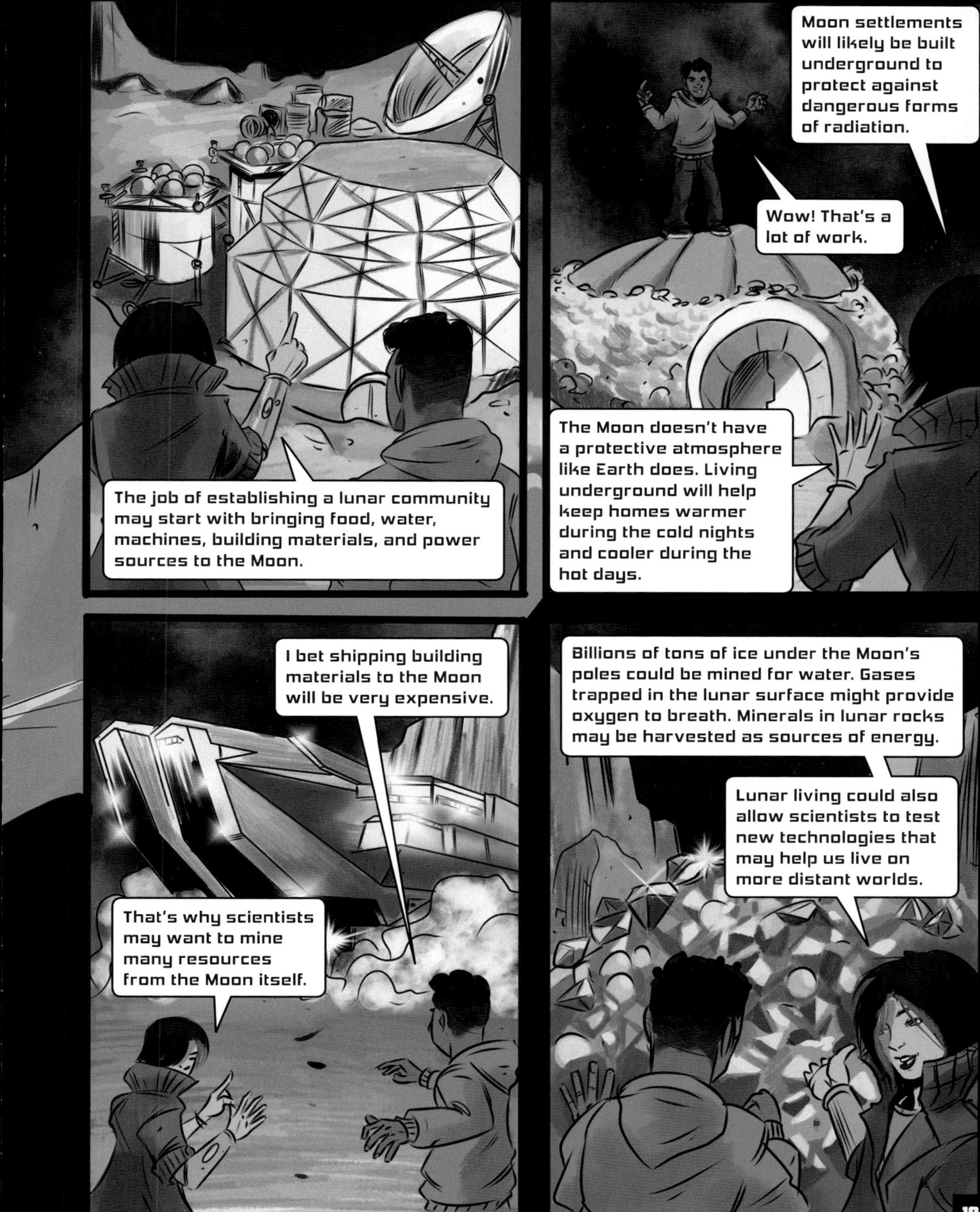
The job of establishing a lunar community may start with bringing food, water, machines, building materials, and power sources to the Moon.
Moon settlements will likely be built underground to protect against dangerous forms of radiation.
Wow! That's a lot of work.
The Moon doesn't have a protective atmosphere like Earth does. Living underground will help keep homes warmer during the cold nights and cooler during the hot days.
I bet shipping building materials to the Moon will be very expensive.
That's why scientists may want to mine many resources from the Moon itself.
Billions of tons of ice under the Moon's poles could be mined for water. Gases trapped in the lunar surface might provide oxygen to breath. Minerals in lunar rocks may be harvested as sources of energy.
Lunar living could also allow scientists to test new technologies that may help us live on more distant worlds.

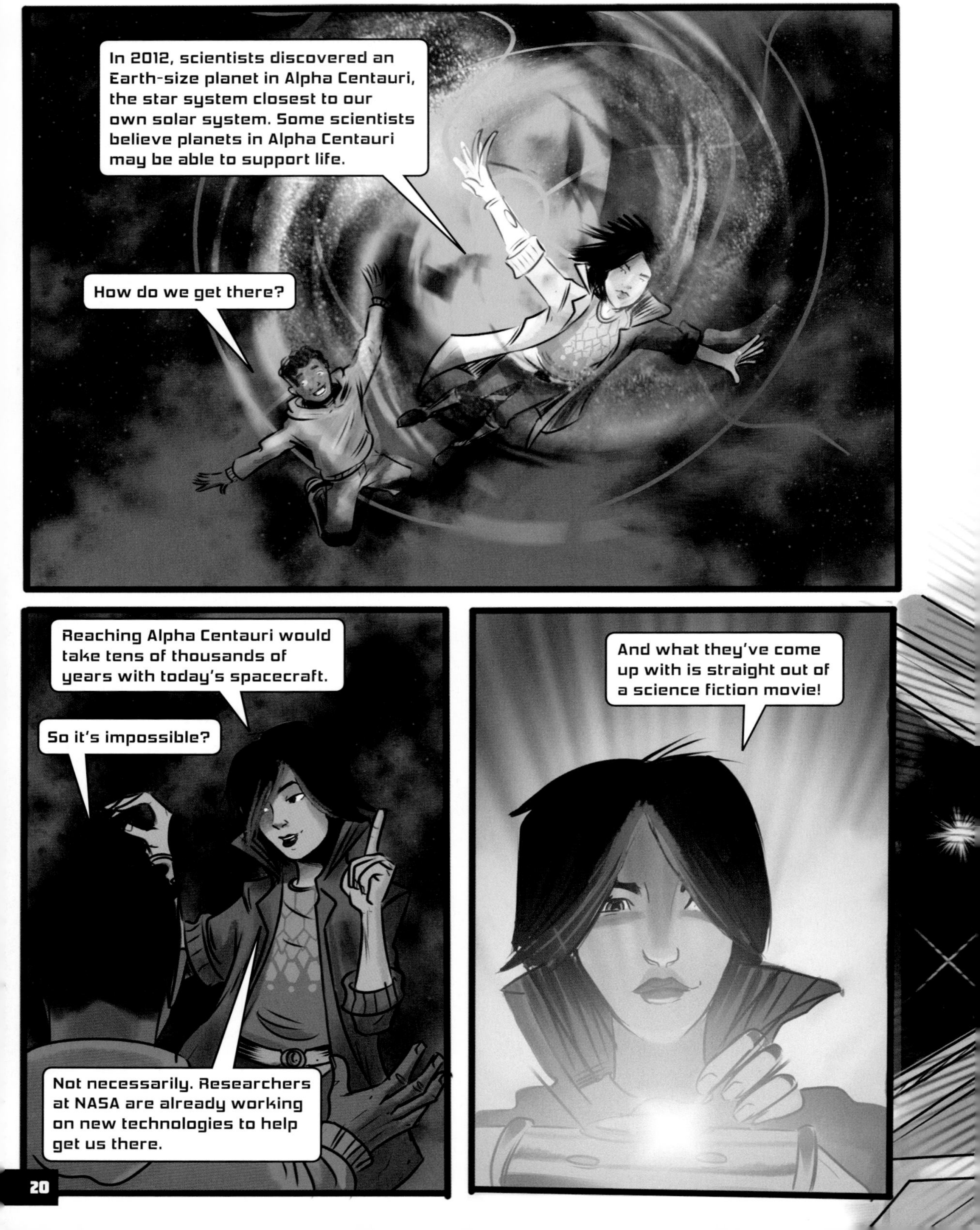
In 2012, scientists discovered an Earth-size planet in Alpha Centauri, the star system closest to our own solar system. Some scientists believe planets in Alpha Centauri may be able to support life.
How do we get there?
Reaching Alpha Centauri would take tens of thousands of years with today's spacecraft.
So it's impossible?
Not necessarily. Researchers at NASA are already working on new technologies to help get us there.
And what they've come up with is straight out of a science fiction movie!

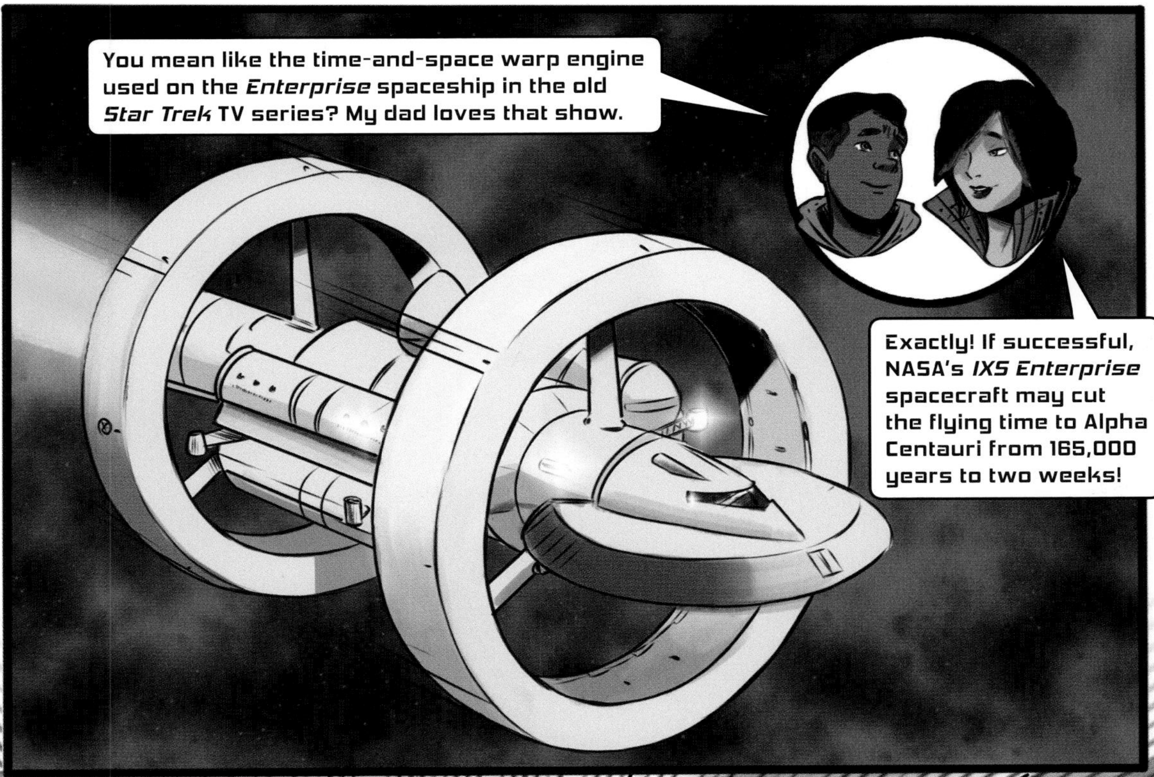
You mean like the time-and-space warp engine used on the *Enterprise* spaceship in the old *Star Trek* TV series? My dad loves that show.
Exactly! If successful, NASA's *IXS Enterprise* spacecraft may cut the flying time to Alpha Centauri from 165,000 years to two weeks!

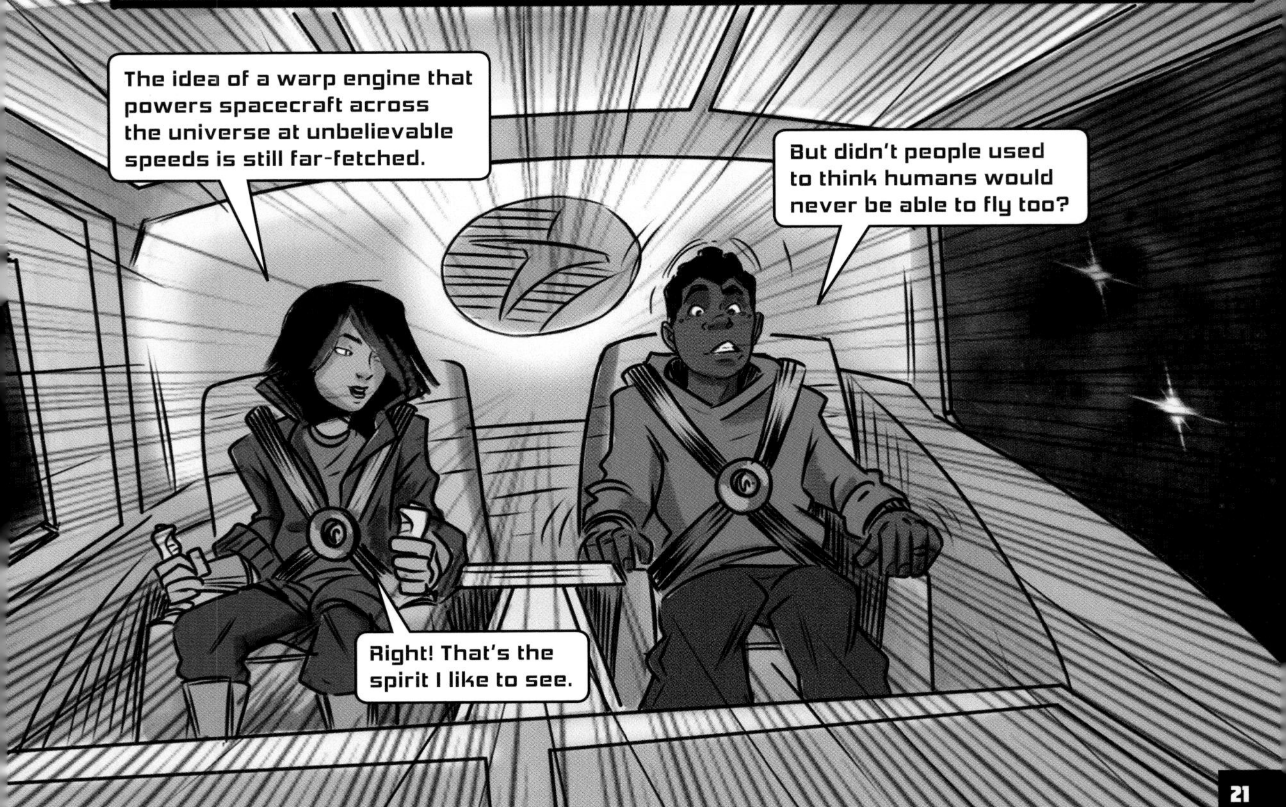
The idea of a warp engine that powers spacecraft across the universe at unbelievable speeds is still far-fetched.
But didn't people used to think humans would never be able to fly too?
Right! That's the spirit I like to see.

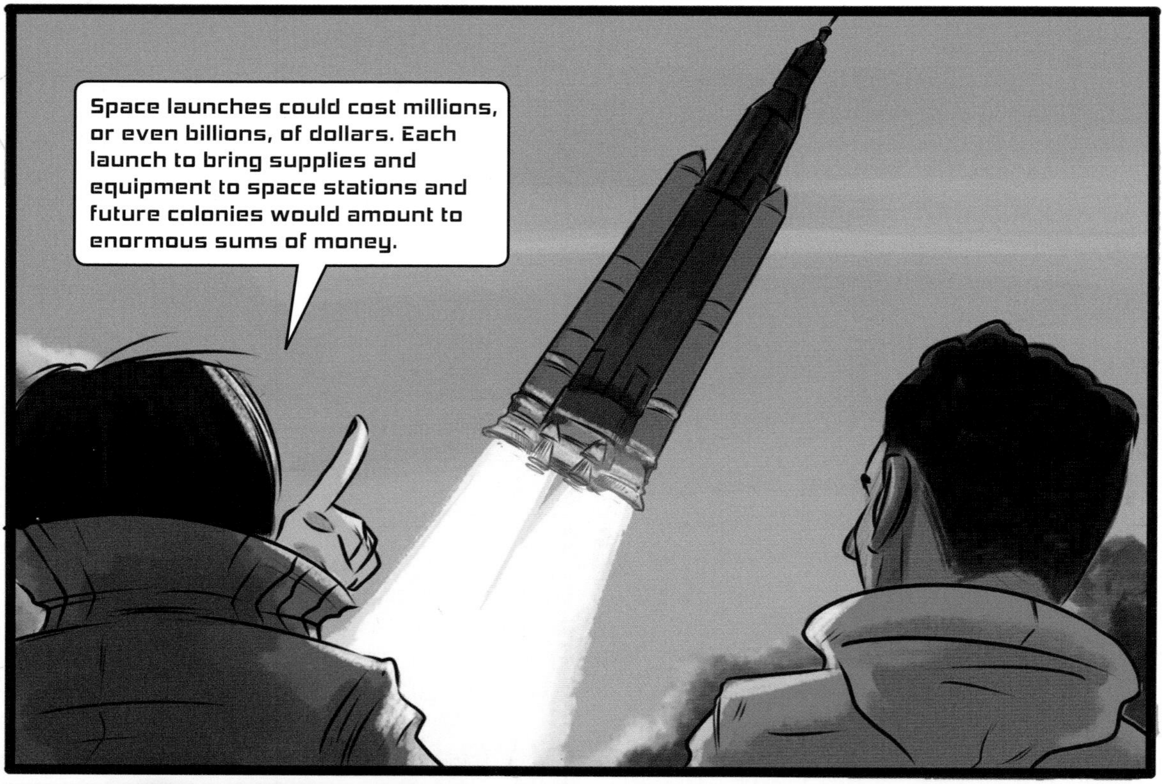
Space launches could cost millions, or even billions, of dollars. Each launch to bring supplies and equipment to space stations and future colonies would amount to enormous sums of money.

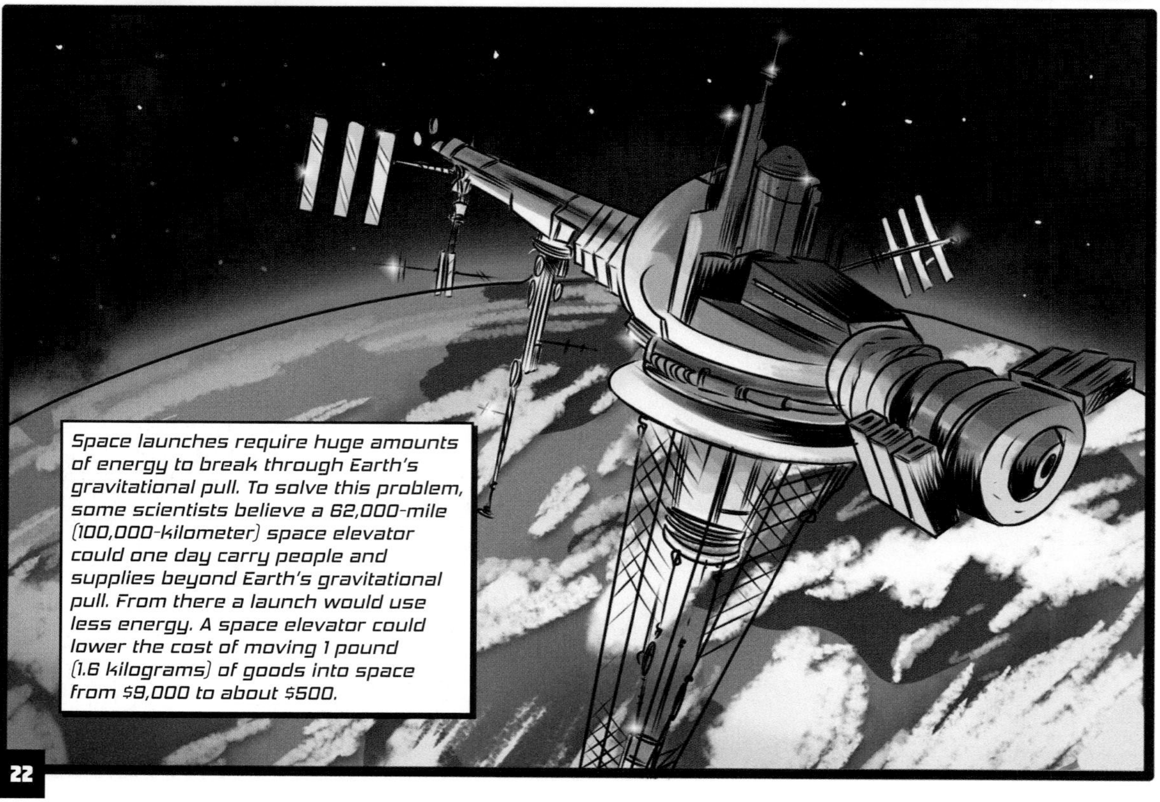
Space launches require huge amounts of energy to break through Earth's gravitational pull. To solve this problem, some scientists believe a 62,000-mile (100,000-kilometer) space elevator could one day carry people and supplies beyond Earth's gravitational pull. From there a launch would use less energy. A space elevator could lower the cost of moving 1 pound (1.6 kilograms) of goods into space from $9,000 to about $500.

The heart of the elevator is a thin tube-like ribbon made of a carbon substance. The idea is that this flexible ribbon would be 100 times stronger than steel.

How would it get into space?

It would be wound into a ball and launched into orbit. Once there, it would unwind and fall back to Earth.

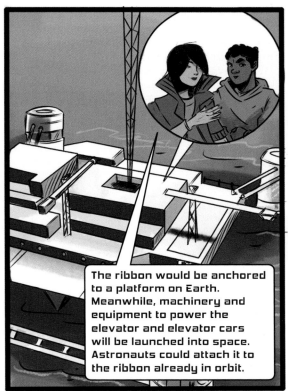

The ribbon would be anchored to a platform on Earth. Meanwhile, machinery and equipment to power the elevator and elevator cars will be launched into space. Astronauts could attach it to the ribbon already in orbit.

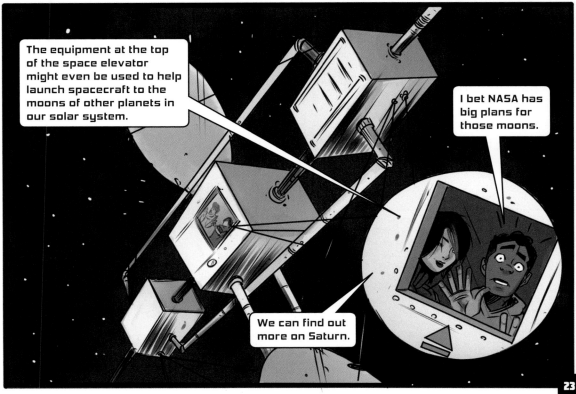

The equipment at the top of the space elevator might even be used to help launch spacecraft to the moons of other planets in our solar system.

I bet NASA has big plans for those moons.

We can find out more on Saturn.

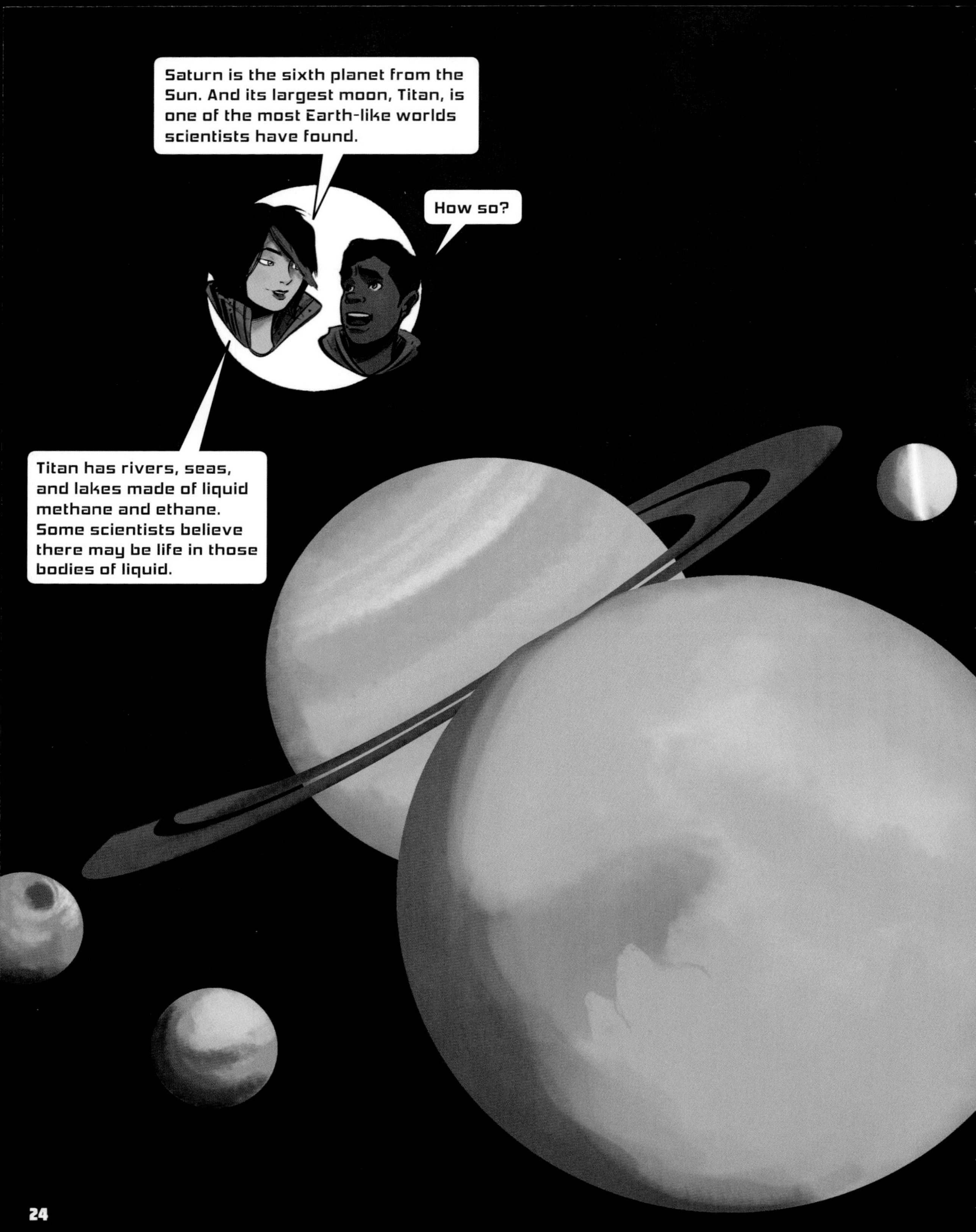
Saturn is the sixth planet from the Sun. And its largest moon, Titan, is one of the most Earth-like worlds scientists have found.
How so?
Titan has rivers, seas, and lakes made of liquid methane and ethane. Some scientists believe there may be life in those bodies of liquid.

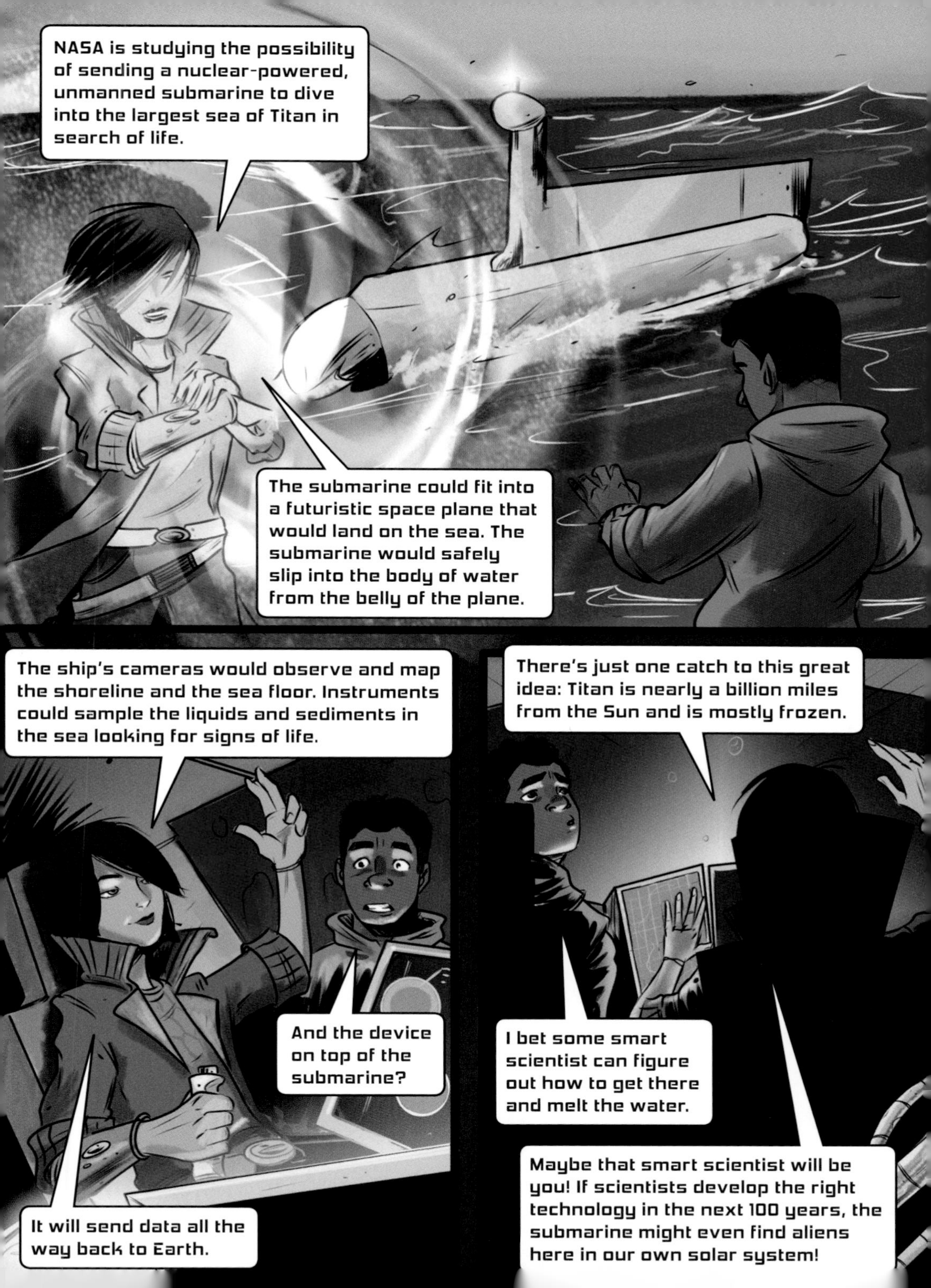
NASA is studying the possibility of sending a nuclear-powered, unmanned submarine to dive into the largest sea of Titan in search of life.
The submarine could fit into a futuristic space plane that would land on the sea. The submarine would safely slip into the body of water from the belly of the plane.
The ship's cameras would observe and map the shoreline and the sea floor. Instruments could sample the liquids and sediments in the sea looking for signs of life.
And the device on top of the submarine?
It will send data all the way back to Earth.
There's just one catch to this great idea: Titan is nearly a billion miles from the Sun and is mostly frozen.
I bet some smart scientist can figure out how to get there and melt the water.
Maybe that smart scientist will be you! If scientists develop the right technology in the next 100 years, the submarine might even find aliens here in our own solar system!

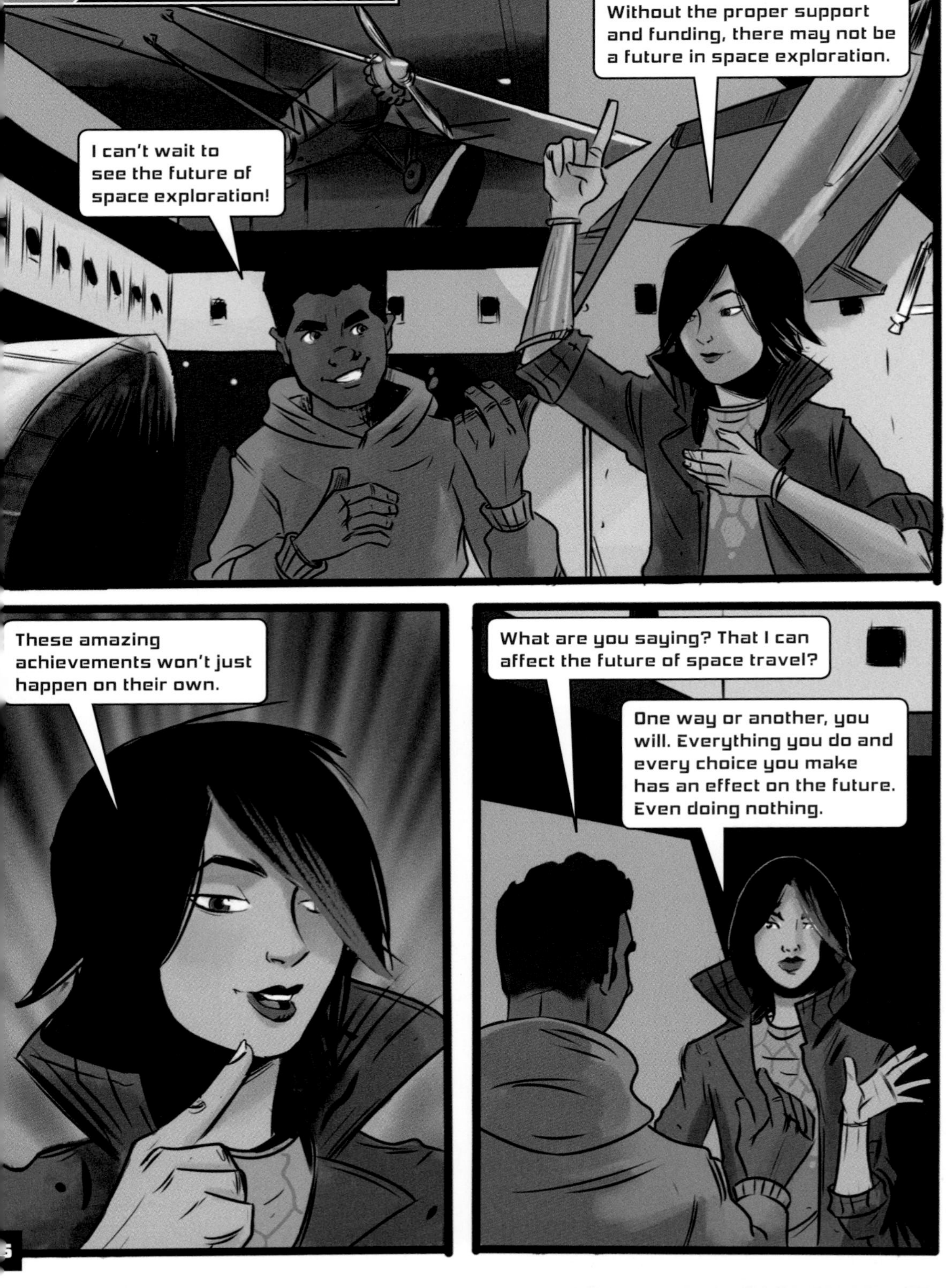
I can't wait to see the future of space exploration!
None of this is certain, Ron. Without the proper support and funding, there may not be a future in space exploration.
These amazing achievements won't just happen on their own.
What are you saying? That I can affect the future of space travel?
One way or another, you will. Everything you do and every choice you make has an effect on the future. Even doing nothing.

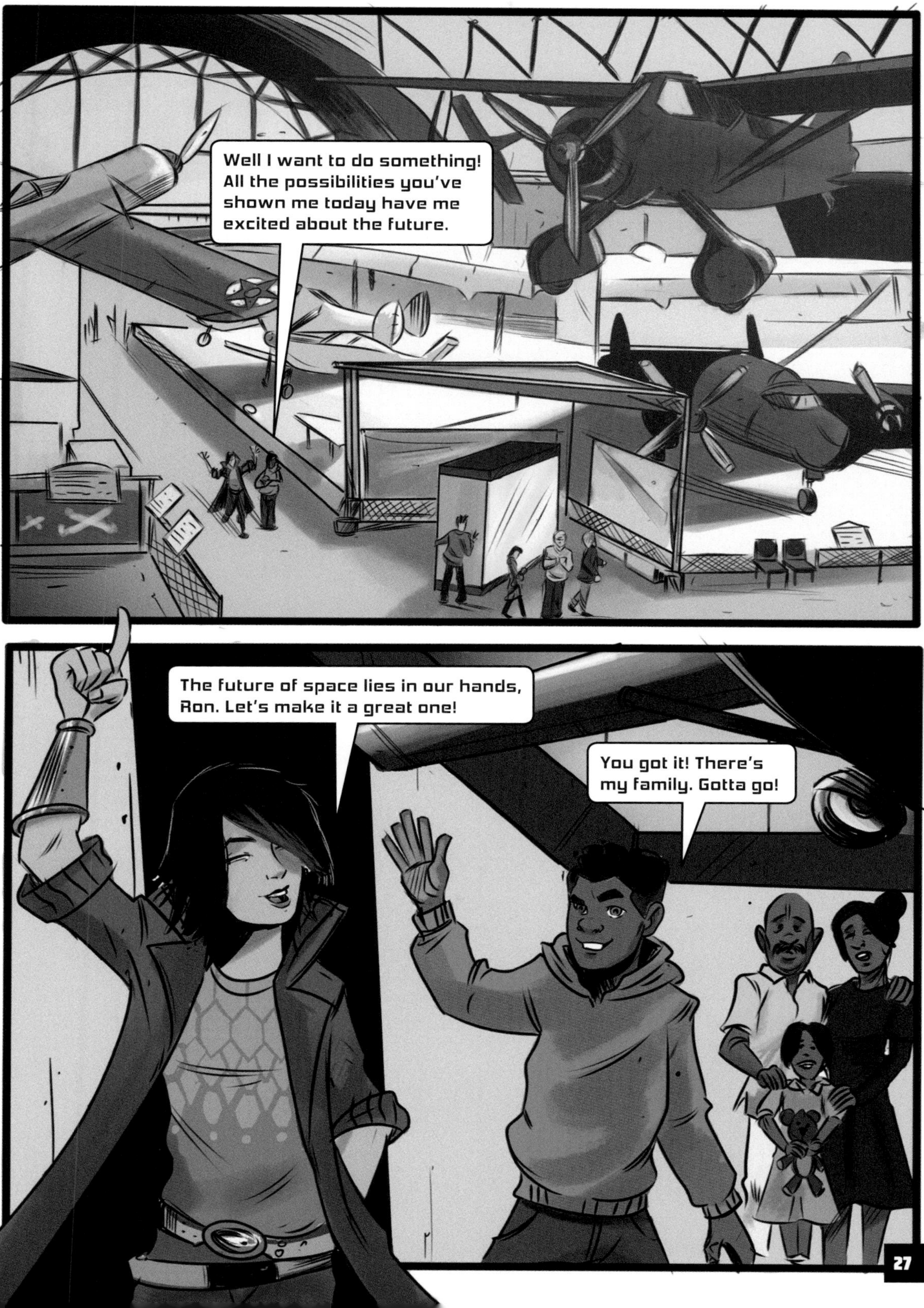
Well I want to do something! All the possibilities you've shown me today have me excited about the future.
The future of space lies in our hands, Ron. Let's make it a great one!
You got it! There's my family. Gotta go!

SPACE EXPLORATION

The term "astronaut" comes from the Greek words *stron*, meaning "star," and *nautes*, meaning "sailor."

On July 20, 1969, Neil Armstrong and Edwin "Buzz" Aldrin became the first humans to reach the Moon. Their *Apollo 11* spacecraft touched down in a flat stretch of land named the Sea of Tranquility.

Astronauts who have taken space walks say space smells like fried steak, raspberries, or burning metal.

The 135th and final mission of the U.S. Space Shuttle program was flown in July 2011. It used the Space Shuttle *Atlantis*.

The *International Space Station* weighs about 925,000 pounds (420 metric tons). That's equal to about 320 automobiles.

The James Webb Space Telescope is NASA's next orbiting space observatory. It will be the successor to the Hubble Space Telescope and is scheduled to launch in October 2018.

You become taller in space. With less gravity pulling down on your body, your spine straightens out. You can become as much as 2 inches (5 cm) taller in space.

In 1970, *Apollo 13* was headed to the Moon when an onboard explosion caused major problems. The astronauts fixed the problems with materials in the craft and returned to Earth safely.

Mars is home to the tallest mountain in our solar system. Olympus Mons, a volcano, is nearly 69,000 feet (21 km) high and 2 million feet (600 km) across! The tallest mountain on Earth is Mount Everest, at 29,035 feet (8,850 meters).

The first woman in space was Russian. Valentine Tereshkova made her historic flight in 1963 on the *Vostock 6* mission. Ms. Tereshkova orbited the Earth 48 times during her nearly 71-hour journey into space.

MORE ABOUT LUNA LI

Futurists are scientists who systematically study and explore possibilities about the future of human society and life on Earth. Luna Li proved herself to be brilliant in this field at a young age. She excelled in STEM subjects and earned her PhD in Alternative Futures from the University of Hawaii at Manoa. Luna invented a gadget she calls the Future Scenario Generator (FSG) that she wears on her wrist. Luna inputs current and predicted data into the FSG. It then crunches the numbers and creates a portal to at holographic reality that humans can enter and interact with.

artificial satellite (ahr-tuh-FISH-uhl SAT-uh-lite)—a human-made craft placed in orbit around a planet or moon in order to collect information

asteroid (AS-tuh-roid)—a rocky object that travels around the Sun

cosmonaut (KOZ-muh-nawt)—an astronaut from Russia

engineer (en-juh-NEERZ)—people who are specially trained to design and build machines or large structures

galaxies (GAL-uhk-seez)—very large groups of stars and planets

holograph (HAH-luh-graf)—an image made by laser beams that looks as if it has depth and dimension

missile (MIS-uhl)—a weapon that is aimed at a target

portal (POR-tuhl)—a doorway or an entrance

radiation (ray-dee-AY-shuhn)—tiny particles sent out from radioactive material

rover (ROE-vur)—a vehicle used to explore the terrain of a planet or its moons

sediment (SED-uh-muhnt)—sand, mud, and other particles produced from weathering

Bailey, Diane. *The Future of Space Exploration.* What's Next? Mankato, Minn.: Creative Education, 2013.

Paris, Stephanie. *21st Century: Mysteries of Deep Space.* Time for Kids Nonfiction Readers. Huntington Beach, Calif.: Teacher Created Materials, 2013.

Rooney, Anne. *Space Record Breakers.* London, UK: Carlton Kids, 2014.

Siy, Alexandra. *Cars on Mars: Roving the Red Planet.* Watertown, Mass.: Charlesbridge, 2011.

INTERNET SITES

FactHound offers a safe, fun way to find Internet sites related to this book. All sites on FactHound have been researched by our staff.

Here's all you do:

Visit *www.facthound.com*

Type in this code: 9781491482650

Super-cool stuff!

Check out projects, games and lots more at
www.capstonekids.com

INDEX